FAITH STRETCHED WITHOUT LIMITS

Taneisha L. Naylor

Preface

I am super excited to release this new book. It is a different creative project that I feel God has compelled me to write. This book is compiled with my thoughts, ideas, life experiences, scriptures, and revelation given to me from the Holy Spirit.

Throughout my twenty-seven years of living and my last five years counseling, coaching, and mentoring hundreds of people, I have come in contact with many powerful stories and people. I've learned over time God connected me with these individuals because they wanted more in life but they all lacked the hope and wisdom that was needed to get to the place they desired to be.

I decided to write this book to impart hope, motivation, and wisdom from God himself in a creative and unique way. Some of what you will read is things I have personally experienced, and other things are from examples I've encountered.

I know what you are thinking. She is only twenty-eight years old. What can she possibly teach me or tell me that I don't know? Let me answer that for you. A person can only learn if they are willing. Firstly, you have to come to grips that you don't know everything. Secondly, you have to accept the fact that everyone can teach you something. Lastly, you have to be willing to receive the knowledge.

Then apply what you've obtained to your everyday life.

This book was not written strictly for motivation or encouragement but to bring you into a deeper level of assurance that you can live an abundant life walking by completely trusting God. As you flip through these pages, the Holy Spirit will speak to you. Your confidence will increase through every word on every page. Your mindset will be transformed. You will understand the identity that God has given you—a child of God who doesn't lack anything and has more than enough.

In spite of all that you have been through and/or the decisions you have made, God still has greater plans for you. Does that surprise you? It surprised me at one stage in my life. I could not get past all that I had done wrong to be able to receive all that God has for me and all that God has to say about me. Well, I want to remind you that God thinks the world of you. He loves you and adores you. You are His creation. He made you. He will do whatever He needs to do to get your attention. To save you. To speak to you. To heal you. To give you the world. So ask yourself why God would hate you or think otherwise of you because of a mistake you made.

We allow our thoughts about ourselves and what the devil tries to whisper in our minds create the way we view ourselves. We come into agreement with these thoughts and perspectives and subconsciously block God out of our minds and thoughts. We do this without even realizing it a lot of times. This limits God from being who He needs to be in our lives. How do you feel about yourself based on the last bad decision you made or based on where you are in life right now? Most people begin to feel, think, and say negative things about themselves, such as "I'm stupid. I'm dumb. I'll always be broke. Things will never get better..."

I am going to challenge as you read to speak the word of God over your life. Coming into agreement with negative type of thinking keeps you in the place you are currently, lacking. This book will stretch you without limits in your thinking and beliefs, which should allow you to live the abundant life God created you for.

Table of Contents

Introduction

Live the Life You've Dreamed Of!

"Twenty years from now you will be more disappointed by the things that you didn't do than by the ones you did do. So throw off the bowlines. Sail away from the safe harbor. Catch the trade winds in your sails. Explore. Dream. Discover." Mark Twain

You typically never forget those big dreams you had as a kid. Think back to when you were a child, riding down the street in the backseat of a car, you looked out the window at other cars and houses and dreamed about one day driving a fancy car and living in a big house. You saw families laughing and playing catch. Parents frolicking with their children in their front yards. Adults driving around in freshly shined cars with the tops down, without any cares in the world.

Meanwhile, you're taking a five-hour drive to the penitentiary to visit a father you haven't seen since you were a newborn. Your mom is in the car telling you she's not sure if she can afford to send you on that ten-dollar field trip at school the following week. She also isn't sure how she's going to pay the month's rent. All you hear are complaints about not having enough money to make ends meet and strategizing ways to scam the system in order to live comfortably.

You sit back and think, *There has to be more to life.* With your head against the backseat, you relax and soon fall asleep for the rest of the ride to the penitentiary. As you're asleep, you go on an amazing journey in your dream.

You see yourself hop from a beautiful all-white Rolls-Royce Phantom to grab your shopping bags from the trunk. You stand before a gigantic beautiful all-white house with ten windows on the front. Four foreign vehicles and two motorcycles are parked in the driveway, which loops around from one end of the sidewalk to the opposite side of the sidewalk, making a semi-circle. The lawn looks like the lawns in Beverly Hills, with lilies, hydrangeas, and orchids.

When you walk into the house, you hear the voices of your spouse and young children. Your spouse, smelling wonderful with that special fragrance you bought him or her for Christmas, greets you with warm kisses and hugs, telling you how much you were missed. Everything inside the house is white and spotless—no stains, dirt, or dust anywhere. It's been cleaned perfectly, just as you like it. You smell the fresh island orchid scent of your favorite candles. Three children, with so much happiness in their hearts, run down the hall with their arms opened wide, eyes glowing to see you. You take the time to embrace and love on them with all that you have. Family means everything to you. This is what you've wanted your future family and life to be. Beautiful, loving, elegant, peaceful, serene, and full of joy.

You walk into the kitchen, toward the island to pour something to drink. Your eyes come across *Essence* magazine, and you spot yourself and your family on the front cover. With excitement and gratitude, tears flow. The words read, "One of the wealthiest families in America" and "Well-known trailblazer." In complete silence, you soak in the moment. As you turn around, your spouse grabs you and experiences this moment with you. You're feeling overwhelmed with emotions and thoughts of happiness. Out loud, you tell God, "These are your promises proving true. Thank you." Suddenly, this dream ends and another one begins.

You're sitting at an office desk in what appears to be your house, looking over bank statements. You come across monthly payments made to local and national non-profit organizations for million dollars each. These non-profits provide resources and assistance to underprivileged children and families around the world. You're all about seeing a big, positive change in the world, helping to eradicate homelessness, and helping those who are struggling. This is a burden you've carried since you were a young child.

Next thing you know, this dream is interrupted because your mom is yelling at you to wake up. You've finally arrived at the penitentiary to see your father, but you're still caught up in this amazing dream, and it's hard for you to move because you're thinking about your wonderful life in the dreams. You feel as if you were at the movies, watching previews to the upcoming TD Jakes film and you were waiting for the next scene.

This dream was mind-blowing. You don't have family or friends who live like this. Everyone you know either lives in the hood or in low-income housing. The excitement to live the life beyond your everyday reality was ignited in you at that moment. Walking into the penitentiary, you have a huge smile on your face. You are not smiling because you are happy to see your father for the first time in over eight years but because of the dream you just experienced. The dream feels so real that you immediately believe that it will be your reality one day.

I've learned if the dream isn't bigger than you, then it's not from God. Your dreams need to be so big they require God to make it possible. Your dreams should scare you. They should make you feel like it's impossible and crazy. Honestly, our brains aren't large enough to have such intricate dreams. If you're not dreaming or have lost all hope to dreaming, I pray you ask God to light something on the inside of you to dream again. I pray your mind is decluttered from negativity and hopelessness

4

and that your hope is ignited. I pray for supernatural access to spiritual revelation from God to be released to you while you're sleep, through dreams and while you're awake through visions.

Breaking Up With the Poverty Mindset

Your abundance depends on your mindset. You can go further than you currently believe you have the ability to go. I grew up in what I consider a big family. I had three brothers and one sister. My biological father was in and out of the prison system from the time I was born into my adult years. So he did not provide any financial assistance to my mom. She was the sole provider, which caused her to qualify for government assistance. This assistance included free public education, free school lunch, food stamps, low-income housing, and section 8 housing. This was a great help to my family. I grew to learn the ins and outs of the government assistance system all too well. It was a topic that was talked about quite often amongst the people in my community. I would hear some of the older adults teaching the younger adults how to qualify and sustain their government assistance. I would listen to these conversations, and unknowingly, the seeds were being planted in me. I grew to understand the ins and outs of obtaining government assistance and how to keep it.

When I began college, I applied to receive a link card. A link card in Illinois is provided by the government to those who qualify to purchase a certain amount of groceries each month. According to the government, I made too much money so I wasn't approved. I think back to that moment when I thought I was going to receive it only to be denied. My feelings were hurt, and I felt let down. I had listened to all those conversations growing up and properly noted how to have a government assistance success story like my community members who were schooled by the elders to receive government assistance. When I was denied, I thought I did something wrong but in reality the qualifications over the years to receive government assistance had changed.

It's crazy how upset I was that I didn't qualify. I was mad at the government, Sally Mae, the white man, and everyone else. When I think about my mindset at the time and my feelings concerning the situation, it makes me nauseous because that was a terrible mindset to have. No one should live their lives with such high expectations to get on government assistance.

I remember telling others around me that I didn't get approved, and they, too, became angry at the government, Sally Mae, and the white man. They proceeded to tell me the updated steps I needed to take so when I reapplied, I would get approved. One of the steps was to cut back on the amount of hours I worked at my job. This was going to be hard for me because I've always had a crazy work ethic and was currently working a lot of overtime. I truly enjoyed working and was attached to the income I received. At the time, I was nineteen years old in a management position at White Castle and I had a part-time job. I was eating well, literally and figuratively. Financially, I was better than straight. I just had the wrong mindset and wanted the government to give me a link card to pay for my food.

I'm sure you can relate to this in some way. Either you've been on government assistance or you've known someone who received a link card, lived in low-income housing, and/or section 8. (Section 8 is the payment assistance for rental housing to low-income families in the United States.) According to the United States Census Bureau, in 2016 there were 40.6 million people in poverty. This number is outstanding and ridiculous. This number is so high because we as a people have come into agreement with the spirit of poverty. Some of you think this is the only level you have access to. Some choose to do nothing with your lives, accept government assistance, and do whatever it takes to stay qualified for it.

I am a believer in receiving government assistance if and when you need it. I'm a firm believer in accessing the resources that you have and need. I've been assisted plenty of times by the government and assistance-based programs. The point I'm making is that we can't become comfortable by settling for government assistance and living below average. We need to think, believe, and work toward greater.

Sadly, these seeds were planted in us by the government for the sole purpose of us staying in poverty and living in fear outside of their assistance. They want you to think we can't make it without them. Most of you have grabbed hold of this mindset and live your life according to it. This is a mindset you need to break up with, and the only way to do this is to see yourself beyond poverty. See yourself beyond government assistance. See yourself living your dream, with your dream family, house, cars, and career. You don't have to be broke. Being broke is a mindset. Living check-to-check and in lack is a mindset.

God has given you gifts, talents, abilities, and experiences that will allow you to get yourself out of poverty. You just have to tap into the wisdom and leading of the Holy Spirit. In order to completely rid yourself of the poverty mindset, you must live your life on the foundation of faith and truly trust God in all things. Faith pushes you into new places, realms, and dimensions that fear can't take you. Once you break up with the spirits of fear and poverty, you will experience the fullness of God. *When you take God out of a box, you will be able to experience the fullness of Him. You will be able to see the God of the universe who owns everything, Adonai.*

Now listen to what God has to say:

I'm All You Need

I need you to trust me.
I need you to listen to my wisdom.
I need you to listen to my instructions.
I need you to obey me.
I need you to have faith in me.
I am trying to change your perspective but you're fighting me.
Stop resisting the shift I am releasing.
Allow me to walk with you.
Allow me to talk to you.
Allow me to love you.
Allow me to show you how I've never left you.
Allow me to show you your purpose.
Allow me to break you.
Allow me to shape you.
Allow me to mold you.
Allow me to grow you.
Allow me to water you.
Allow me to feed you.
Allow me to lead you.
Allow me to guide you.
Allow me to take you places you've never been.
Allow me to take you deeper than you've ever wondered.
Allow me to help you walk on water.
Allow me to take you to where you've always desired to go.

Follow me.
I'm all you need.
I'm Adonai.

The Vision Will Manifest

"Write the vision; make it plain on tablets, so he may run who reads it" (Habakuk 2:2, The English Standard Version).

Imagine walking into a room with elegant furniture, beautiful portraits on the walls, and sparkling chandeliers hanging from the ceiling. The more you walk and look around the room you notice familiar faces and unfamiliar ones. Everyone claps and cheers you on as you strut in with your bomb-fitted red Givenchy dress as if you're Beyoncé on the red carpet at the Met Gala. Some people shout "congratulations" while others yell "I'm proud of you." You're smiling from ear to ear, saying "thank you all" and embracing people when they come up to hug you. You are amazed by the moment. As you take your seat, an extreme level of gratitude hits you. Your eyes fill with tears as you soak in and enjoy the moment. NO one has ever celebrated you to this magnitude before. You feel as if you're in a movie scene.

As you take a few moments to yourself, you contemplate on what it took for you to get to this place. Your eyes are filled with tears that can't stop flowing. It hits you. This is the manifestation of the vision you wrote down and declared long ago. You're in amazement it actually came to past.

Do you know that we have the ability to create visions and ideas and with God we have the power to bring them to life? Our minds are powerful and creative. That's the way God wired us. I have created many visions, written them down, believed they would come to pass, worked toward it, and they did.

Today, before I sat down to write, I had never thought of the vision I wrote about above. It wasn't until I walked into a beautiful restaurant that the Lord revealed this to me. I dug deeper and asked God what was He saying and why was He revealing this. The Lord said He wanted me to write this down and share it with the readers of this book, in order for you to create a future vision for your life. A vision that is bigger than you. One that takes God to manifest.

What do you desire life to look like one day? What is something so big that you are working on or preparing to work on? Take a few minutes and ask God for that vision. What will the end result be? What will it look like? Give details. Talk about your surroundings. Talk about your feelings, your thoughts, and whatever else is on your mind. Write this down. This could be your future wedding or giving birth to your beautiful child. You might want to be a teacher, singer, or author.

Maybe you want to graduate with a degree or hope your family comes together.

God gave me this celebratory vision, particularly so you would know to celebrate along the journey. This is imperative. Many times, we focus so much on walking in our purpose and helping others that we forget to celebrate ourselves. Celebrating yourself can be as simple as going out for an evening, enjoying time with friends, or taking a personal day to do nothing. This will help you think clearer and hopefully get you in the habit of celebrating life. There are too many not-so-good occurrences in life, and we need to ensure we are not spending all our time focusing on those. Instead, spend time celebrating yourself and others.

Now create a vision:

_____
_____
_____
_____
_____
_____
_____
_____
_____
_____
_____
_____
_____
_____
_____
_____
_____
_____
_____
_____
_____
_____
_____
_____
_____
_____
_____
_____
_____
_____

Created To Succeed

"Commit your actions to the LORD, and your plans will succeed" (Proverbs 16:3, New Living Translation).

Did you know you cannot fail with God? God knew you before you were formed in your mother's womb. He thought of you. He created you. He put together all the details of your life. He knitted and wove every piece of you together—everything including experiences, DNA, skin color, features, gifts, abilities, purpose, residences, and the family you were born into. Even the very hairs on your head are all numbered (Luke 12:7). They are all a part of God's sole purpose to your success. He knew all that you would do and every mistake you would make. This still did not stop Him from dying for you and giving you a purpose.

You will be able to live in your true purpose once you come to believe and receive that you were created to succeed in whatever you choose to do, and that the light will shine on the road ahead of you (Job 22:28, New International Version). God said it, not I.

Now say this out loud to God:

Failure is not an option

No longer will I question you.
No longer will I be impatient with you.

I will trust you.
I will believe everything that you have told me.

I trust and believe that I will succeed.
I believe that I am called to greatness.

I will run and not be weary.
I will walk and will not give up.

I will go wherever you want me to go.
I will do whatever you want to me to do.
I will say whatever you want me to say.

I know that I will not fail.

I will walk boldly.
I will walk confidently.
I will walk by faith and not by sight.

I see the light.
I see the bigger picture.
I see glimpses of my future.

No longer will I question you.

I will trust you.

I trust you because you are worthy.

I will trust you because your plans are greater than my own.

I trust you because you created me in your image.

You created me to succeed.
In Jesus name, Amen.

Boxed In

"Now unto him that is able to do exceeding abundantly above all that we ask or think, according to the power that worketh in us" (Ephesians 3: 20, King James Version).

Everything changed for me when I came into the real knowledge and understanding that I will succeed at whatever God created me to do. In one year alone, I've seen the power of God in my life like never before due to my trust in Him. In my past, I didn't used to be as confident in God as I am now. When I began to completely trust Him, everything in my life drastically changed for the better.

I want you to believe and receive that you were created to succeed. Success is not measured by the amount of money you make, the people you know, or the title you hold. Success is measured by your reliance and obedience to God. This allows you to walk entirely in your purpose so you can receive all that God has for you.

Most people buy boxes when it's time to move out of their houses, when they need to put things in storage, or when they want to wrap gifts. And not all gifts are wrapped in boxes. When you think about it, boxes are commonly used to store things or move things from one place to another. Boxes have limitations. There is only so much space to fit things in a box. You need to measure the box's dimensions to see what can actually fit. You can't fit a car into an 8x10 box. You can't fit a refrigerator into a 10x12 box. Both of these things are impossible because the items are larger than the boxes.

Most times we put God in a box and keep Him there. Why is it we try to fit God in boxes when He is larger and greater than any box? Let's stop putting God in boxes so we can have access to all that He has for our lives. We were not created to live in lack or fear, so why do we end up there? This is due to the limitations we place on God. We claim to be believers, but our faith is the size of an engagement ring box. It's not large enough to hold or store all the blessings God have for our lives.

As you continue reading this book, you will be inspired to make changes—mentally, emotionally, physically, and spiritually. These changes will result in removal of fear and lack. You will come into a deeper revelation of what it means to have complete reliance on God and become equipped to live a life stretched without limits.

Complete Confidence

According to Merriam-Webster, the definition of <u>faith</u> is:

1. Complete trust or confidence in someone or something.

2. Strong belief in God or in the doctrines of a religion, based on spiritual   apprehension rather than proof.

Biblically speaking, we can't talk about faith and not include the Father of faith himself, Abraham. Abraham's life is a true testament of one who walks by the definition of faith. He had complete trust in God. His confidence in what God told Him to do is a great example of how our confidence should be in God and His leading in our very lives.

As a child, God used my family to speak prosperity over my life. There were words spoken over me that one day I would become "somebody" and be "successful."

One of my brothers used to say, "Neisha gone be somebody," and "If ain't nobody else gone be nothing, we know Neisha is." My mother used to say, "My baby is an entrepreneur."

I thank God for using them as vessels to declare His plans over my life. At the time, they didn't know what they were doing. I don't think they realized the power over the words they spoke and that God used them to say those things. However, to this day I'm very thankful for their obedience in those moments.

Since those seeds were planted in me at such an early age, unknowingly I developed trust in God that I would see those words come to pass. I grew up with confidence that I was going to be "somebody" and that one day I would be an entrepreneur. This allowed me to have big dreams as a child. The funny thing is that I didn't know the depth of what those words meant, but I repeated them with much optimism. I had hope those words would become my reality one day, and I clung to them. Even in the darkest moments of my life, those seeds didn't die. I believed with everything in me that one day I would see those very words manifest.

This commendable level of optimism that I had at such a young age was given to me from God. I look back to five-year-old me, and the level of confidence, hope, and optimism I carried blows my mind. The wisdom and depth of my faith at such a young age amazed my family and those who met me. At the time, I didn't realize how uncommon this was for a child. I was just naturally being myself, a child trying to be a child. Nonetheless, when you have certain gifts, abilities, and anointings in your life, you're not normal, and everyone can see and hear how different you are no matter how normal you think you are. I was different from most children my age. My mind, discernment, creativity, entrepreneur acumen, wisdom, love for people, and the pure joy I was graced with weren't normal for children.

I naturally excelled in everything I did. I didn't have to try hard in academics, sports, meeting new people, or getting a job. I did everything with the optimistic mindset that I would succeed. This brings us back to Abraham and how everything he did was attached to his expectation in God. He did not spend time worrying about things that might go wrong. He didn't contemplate obeying the leading of the Lord because it made his flesh uncomfortable. He didn't delay what God was telling him to do because he thought about what others would say. Whatever God told Him to do, he did it without hesitation.

Abraham's faith was not moved due to the promises from God that He knew were connected to his obedience. His faith was moved by his complete confidence in God. Let that bless you. Don't put your faith in the blessings that come from God. Put your faith in God, and blessings will come. God is glorified and exalted due to the faith we have in Him when things seem impossible. You must trust that all good things work for them that love and trust God.

When God asks you to do something that you don't understand and that seems impossible, you have to put your trust in Him and focus on Him. He already has it figured out. Trying to wrap your mind around His plans are seemingly impossible. Your brain doesn't have the capacity to understand the fullness of God and His plans. And trying to do things in your own strength and might will never work. "'Not by might nor by power, but by my Spirit,' says the LORD Almighty" (Zechariah 4:6, NIV).

Be Deliberate About Your Obedience

"[God] said, 'Take your son, your only son Isaac, whom you love, and go to the land of Moriah, and offer him there as a burnt offering on one of the mountains of which I shall tell you.' So Abraham rose early in the morning, saddled his donkey, and took two of his young men with him, and his son Isaac. And he cut the wood for the burnt offering and arose and went to the place of which God had told him" (Genesis 22:2-3, ESV).

Let's take a look at what God instructed Abraham to do:

    A. Take his son and go to the land of Moriah.

    B. Offer him as a burnt offering on one of the mountains of which I shall tell you.

Now let's take a look at what Abraham did deliberately to walk in obedience to God:

    A. Rose early the next morning.

    B. Saddled his donkey.

    C. Took two of his young men with him and his son, Isaac.

D. Cut the wood for the burnt offering.

E. Arose and went to the place of which God had told him.

The instructions from God seem so simple, but they were not. These specific instructions took time, effort, and strength, and I'm sure it was quite emotional for Abraham. He had to go on a journey to offer His son as a burnt offering. However, Abraham didn't let his thoughts or emotions hinder him. He quickly responded to God through obedient measures. His devotion to deliberately obey God every step of the way is an outstanding example for all of us.

He made sure he planned deliberately, strategically, and wisely. He was *deliberate* about planning for his trip—who to bring, what to bring, and what steps to take along the way. With wisdom, Abraham knew he could not complete this assignment on his own, so he was *wise* about bringing two servants with him. Also, he was *strategic* about making sure everything got to their destination so this assignment could be completed properly.

I know most of you reading this would have struggled to intentionally be obedient to these instructions from God, especially because they tug on your emotions. Can you imagine packing up your car with a few items needed for the journey, grabbing two accountability partners to journey with you, waking up early, filling up your gas tank, and head to an unknown place to sacrifice your child? I'm sure it's hard to even think about. But let me remind you that obedience is better than sacrifice. As a result of Abraham's strategic planning, use of wisdom, complete trust in God, and obedience, his faith unlocked Heavenly miracles.

9When they reached the place God had told him about, Abraham built an altar there and arranged the wood on it. He bound his son Isaac and laid him on the altar, on top of the wood. 10Then he reached out his hand and took the knife to slay his son. 11But the angel of the Lord called out to him from heaven, 'Abraham! Abraham!' 'Here I am,' he replied. 12'Do not lay a hand on the boy,' [God] said. 'Do not do anything to him. Now I know that you fear God, because you have not withheld from me your son, your only son.' 13Abraham looked up and there in a thicket he saw a ram caught by its horns. He went over and took the ram and sacrificed it as a burnt offering instead of his son. So Abraham called that place The Lord Will Provide. And to this day it is said, 'On the mountain of the Lord it will be provided.' 15The angel of the Lord called to Abraham from heaven a second time and said, 'I swear by myself, declares the Lord, that because you have done this and have not withheld your son, your only son, I will surely bless you and make your descendants as numerous as the stars in the sky and as the sand on the seashore. Your descendants will take possession of the cities of their enemies, and through your offspring all nations on earth will be blessed, because you have obeyed me' (Genesis 22: 9-15).

Your obedience is connected to blessings for those who are connected to you. If nothing else motivates you to intentionally obey God, let it come from the constant reminder of the prosperity those who are connected to you will receive. When you walk in obedience, you will still fall short. You will not always get everything right nor will you be perfect. This is how God gets glory through our lives. He shows others, as well as ourselves, more of himself through our imperfections. Abraham was not perfect; in fact, he had shortcomings. Don't let your imperfections stop you from receiving what God has for your future.

Say this out loud to God:

Then and Now

Lord, you want me to trust you and not worry.
I want to be transparent with you.
I trust you to do some things in my life but not all things.
I repent for asking you for things and not believing you would really answer me.
I repent for always overthinking things and trying to figure everything out before it happens.
I repent for worrying about things even after you give me peace and wisdom.
I repent for fearing the future.

I repent for half-heartedly believing the things you've promised me.

I repent because I have secretly rushed you to move in certain areas of my life only to make my flesh happy.

I repent because secretly I didn't believe everything you have told me about my future.

I believed you would get me a new car when my old car broke down.

I believed you would feed me when I didn't have money to eat.

I believed you would wake me up every day and give me what I needed to get through the day.

I just couldn't see how you would change my current situation completely.

I just couldn't see how you could heal my broken heart.

I just couldn't see how you would heal my sick body.

I just couldn't see how you could change my living and financial situation.

I just couldn't see how you would make me into a spouse.

I just couldn't see how you could fully heal and restore my family.

I just couldn't see all the plans and the thoughts you have for me.

Now I see you differently.

Now I know you as healer.

Now I know you as way maker.

Now I know you as interrupter.

Now I know you as deliverer.

Now I know you as creator.

Now I know you as God.
Now I will trust you.
Now I will obey you.
Now I walk blindly with you.
In Jesus Name, Amen.

Diamonds Are Formed Under Pressure

As you go through life, God will be with you. He will speak to you, lead you, guide you, protect you, and never forsake you. As you continue to trust and purposely obey Him, the more He will reveal His plans to you.

As you walk in your journey, many processes and many trials will occur. The processes and trials will not be easy. Some will be strenuous, intensive, tough, and overwhelming. Everything in you will tell you to turn in a different direction and give up. Look at it this way: trials are a part of the cleansing and growing process, and they will take away your impurities. Everything that is in you that will hinder, hurt, or kill you needs to be removed. Trials produce knowledge and wisdom that you wouldn't have without going through them.

Let's take a look at the process of a diamond. According to www.diamonds.pro, diamonds are not only formed under the heat and pressure of earth's gravity, but can form in the midst of a collision between earth and an asteroid. Oftentimes, we mistake the importance of heat and pressure in the midst of trials in our life. We don't acknowledge and respect the importance of either, and we tend to waste our time complaining and comparing our processes to those around us. This was never God's intentions for us when going through life's processes. His overall goal was to purify, perfect, and strengthen our faith while using us for His glory.

Your response to trials should turn into "My hope lies in you, God," instead of "Why is something bad always happening with me?" Naturally, you will have a battle in your mind and emotions. Your mind will want you to focus on your feelings, but you can't. During these battles you must hold onto what God has told you and who you know God to be. He is a miracle worker, way maker, light in the darkness, leader, guider, healer, protector, Father, provider, sustainer, and so much more. You should have great expectations in Him alone. Trust that He knows all and plans well. Whatever you do, don't abort the process.

Pressure doesn't always come from the devil, either. We are so quick to call everything the devil. When pressure shows, it is because something great is on the other side. Keep in mind the greatest things are produced under pressure. You will feel like giving up. You will feel tired. You will feel like you have no fight left in you. You will feel like you don't know what to do. When these feelings occur, remember this is normal. The key is not giving up and to let the light that God placed inside of you shine brightly.

What does God want you to know?

My child,
You are covered by the blood. You are safe because of the blood of Jesus Christ. I'm with you, and I want you to know that I will never leave you. I created you to shine. Your light cannot be hidden for any longer. I have plans for you that are greater than your understanding. I only tell you what you can handle. I know you better than you know yourself. Don't get frustrated because you don't have all the answers. Don't give up because you feel lost or hopeless. When those feelings come up, it's important for you to remember that my plans are perfect and they never fail. Yes, there will be some battles that you have to fight. Yes, you will feel some pressure. I knew this before I created you. That's why I equipped you for them. You can withstand the forces and the trials that you will face. I created you to excel as long as you walk with me. You have nothing to worry about. Now GO! Move forward with great confidence in me as your perfect planner and shield. I got you. Love, Dad.

Heart Transplant

Lord, it's been fifty two whole days since the
    worse day of my life
Some days my heart aches
While other days I feel my heart skipping a beat
Some days I feel great
While others I am emotionally wrecked

Most days I rejoice and dance to the music from Heaven

While other days I sit at your feet crying due to the hell I've endured

I just want this pain to be completely over already

I feel my flesh rising some days with impure thoughts

And impure motives

I'm trying to get these crazy thoughts out of my mind

They say a mind thinks what has entered into a man's heart

Cleary my heart has been filtrated with the wrong thoughts

Full of selfish emotions and soulish ambitions

You have given me everything I need to get rid of everything that does not reflect you

I need you to come into my heart and clean it

Remove all of the pain, anger, hate, envy, fears, unforgiveness

And everything that does not reflect you

Just take my whole heart away and give me a new one

God, I know that you can do anything

So I'm asking you for just one thing
A Heart Transplant

The Wind Will Be Against You

I finally had the job I had been praying for. The only issue was, I had to be trained on the job and this required a long commute to work for only God knows how long. I can think of the many below zero, freezing rain and snowy days at the beginning of 2017 that I took a 2 hour drive to DeKalb, IL from Chicago each day for work. The commute was strenuous, not to mention the intense wind that I felt every inch of.

I drive a small, four-door Hyundai Accent, and it would get beat up in the wind each day as I traveled to and from work. Some days, I wanted to turn my car around mid-commute and call off for the day. I knew this was not the right thing to do, so I had to fight my way through the wind and terrible weather conditions to get to my destination.

While at my current job, I was working part-time for myself. My business was growing quickly, and it seemed as if every time I looked up there was so much to do in my own business and in my career. I had moments where I was overwhelmed and contemplated giving it all up. For several late nights and early mornings, with little sleep, I petitioned God, asking Him if I could stop doing everything I was doing at work and in my personal life. I begged Him to make everything easier and give me some slack.

Many days, I contemplated stopping everything I was called to do. I knew I was on assignment at my job. God showed me the reason why I was at my job daily. He showed me why I needed to be connected to every client I worked with, exactly why I was there in that season, and why I had to finish my assignment. He showed me exactly why He wouldn't allow me to quit on my assignment. Not only would I make Him look bad, but I would have to redo the assignment over and over until I passed it.

I will not reveal the name of my employer because that doesn't matter, but I will tell you how much hell I went through. I experienced racism, prejudice, torment, affliction—every type of hell you can think of.

Still, I still went to work with peace, joy, God, and my army of angels.

I would walk around the job:

- Smiling

- Singing the songs of the Lord

- Working hard

- Loving on people who were hard to love

- Praying for people privately and publicly

- Speaking life over the business and coworkers

- Doing assignments my boss gave me at the last minute that weren't in my job description.

At the end of every workday at the office, I used to call my best friend to complain about the hell I endured. I had so much frustration and didn't understand how people could be so angry, malicious, deceitful, envious, jealous, and conniving. I wanted to be a great employee by using my skills, gifts, and abilities to help accomplish the mission of the company. A part of the mission was to positively change lives in the community, and I was uncertain why they were doing everything in hell to negatively change my life.

My boss and coworkers asked me, "What are you singing? We hear you through the walls in our office when you go to the bathroom." With confusion on my face as to why the walls were so doggone thin, I smiled and answered. This interaction became a normalcy around the office. Initially, I was singing and humming softly to show respect to others in the work environment. Once everyone kept asking me what I was singing as if they were really interested, I decided to sing and hum a bit louder when I went to the bathroom.

As I think about this, I'm laughing and I shouldn't be. Honestly, it was ignorance. I had no business increasing the volume no matter the questions or interest they seemed to have in my singing. On the days when ALL HELL broke loose in the office, I would put both earphones in my ears and listen to worship music. I would sing softly, pray, and sing in tongues at my desk. My boss could not stand it when I put the headphones in my ears. My response was the "DO NOT DISTURB" sign that you see on hotel doors. This was my way of showing I didn't want to be added to any drama and that I was protecting myself from any demonic forces, plans, or attacks that would try to throw me off for the day.

Eventually, my training was done. This meant I only had to spend one day in the office per week and I could work from home. I made my own schedule and traveled around the state to meet each of my clients. I loved everything about my job, especially the freedom to work from home four out of five days a week.

While on my daily two-hour commute to work about four months into this job, I was on the phone with a friend complaining I wanted to quit my job because of everything I was enduring. She advised me to stay, be patient, and trust God. She told me that God said, "There will be a 'pop' in the spirit when it is time for you to leave." I received the word of the Lord from her and soaked in it for the rest of my drive to work. After we got off the phone, I asked God what the "pop" was that he had referred to and wasn't I currently feeling the "pop"? I felt every bit of anger, frustration, and uncomfortable feelings from being at this job.

Within the first eight months of working here, I was experiencing headaches with them financially. It got to the point where there were issues with my bi-weekly checks coming on time. This became a consistent thing. It was always excuses: "The bank messed up the deposit;" "We forgot to put in payroll on time;" or "My husband is out sick and can't put in payroll so we will write you a check to pick up from the office this week."

There are five things I don't play about: God, my food, my family, my man, and my money. My employer was playing with my money, and in my mind, this was the "pop" my friend had talked about. But noooooo, God told me I was wrong. That was not the "pop" he was referring to. He told me He was allowing these issues with my checks.

Let me be clear. God was not making sure I didn't receive my checks on time. He doesn't operate like that. The enemy is the one who steals, kills, and destroys. God can stop anything, but He allows unfortunate things to happen to us sometimes. His reasons why are always greater than we can see. There always lessons God designed for us to learn during unfortunate circumstances. In this particular situation, God wanted me to see Him as provider, way maker, sustainer, and promise keeper. He also wanted to use this situation to bring clarity, instructions, and peace to me. God is such a loving and intentional Father. He knows all of us better than we know ourselves. He knows exactly what each of us needs.

26Look at the birds of the air, for they neither sow nor reap nor gather into barns; yet your heavenly Father feeds them. Are you not of more value than they? 27Which of you by worrying can add one cubit to his stature? 28"So why do you worry about clothing? Consider the lilies of the field, how they grow: they neither toil nor spin; 29and yet I say to you that even Solomon in all his glory was not arrayed like one of these.30Now if God so clothes the grass of the field, which today is, and tomorrow is thrown into the oven, will He not much more clothe you, O you of little faith? 31"Therefore do not worry, saying, 'What shall we eat?' or 'What shall we drink?' or 'What shall we wear?' 32For after all these things the Gentiles seek. For your heavenly Father knows that you need all these things. 33But seek first the kingdom of God and His righteousness, and all these things shall be added to you. 34Therefore do not worry about tomorrow, for tomorrow will worry about its own things. Sufficient for the day is its own trouble (Matthew 6:26 KJV).

The checks not coming on time didn't stop God from providing for my needs and making a way out of no way. There were many days when bills and late notices would arrive, but I was never late to the point it affected my credit. God sustained me during those times to show me what He was capable of doing. He could have simply let my checks come on time and let me pay my bills on time without letting Him step in to show me He is a promise keeper and so much more. In Matthew 6:26-34, the Bible talks about not having any worries. It shows us how God takes care of the lilies and the birds and that we don't need to worry about anything because we are more valuable.

After studying this passage of scriptures back in 2012, in one of the hardest seasons of my life, I held on tight to those words. These scriptures allowed for me to gracefully walk through the toughest obstacles and battles in my life. I knew God would take care of me as His daughter. So, when my checks were late, I may have complained and have been stressed in one moment, but then the word came alive in me and I was reminded who my Father in Heaven was.

After being at my job for nine months, one morning I awoke from a very detailed dream. As I sat in my bed asking God for the interpretation of this dream, he gave me the answers right then and there. He showed and told me this dream represented the end of my assignment at my current job and that it was time to be self-employed. This dream was followed by much confirmation from God. It caught me off guard but it was exactly what I needed to hear from God. It was a dream come true. However, I knew it would not be easy working for myself.

I've learned that every obstacle, trial, and test, produces lessons necessary for our growth and development. These lessons teach, prepare, position, and nurture us for what's ahead. You may feel like you're in a place in life where all the odds are against you. You may be complaining about your current season. Everything may appear to be falling apart. Everyone you thought would be there is nowhere to be found. You may have more bills than money. You may be in between blessings or in between jobs. You may be depressed, stressed, frustrated, and ready to give up. You may even have thoughts of aborting your purpose.

I understand exactly where you are. I have been there plenty of times. The important thing is to hold on to God and keep your mind hopeful. Think beyond where you currently are. See yourself in a better place. Pray for yourself to come out of the darkness, guilt, and shame. Believe that God is shifting things as you read this passage. Believe that everything you are going through right now is preparing you for something greater.

Your breakthrough is taking place as you read this. You're about to be in a season where you look back on your past and pinch yourself. You will pinch yourself hard because you can't believe you made it out. Not only did you make it out, you made it out on top. You're right where you desired to be. You're farther than you envisioned. You've made it to the top of the mountain. Now looking down to the bottom of the mountain, you see people traveling up the mountain, people stuck in the same places they've been for a while, and people traveling back down the mountain. You feel their pain. You feel the weight of their obstacles. You hear their cries. You feel their burdens. Now it's your job to help others fight against the wind so they can get to the top as well.

Re-Routed

I left late for work one day
It seemed like everybody and their momma was
    on the road
I was going over the speed limit
Pushing on my gas to make it before every red
    light
I had less than twenty minutes to get to work
I jumped on the expressway
As soon as I got on, traffic was bumper to bumper
I typed my address into the gps to see how long it
    would take me to get to work
Gps pulled up three different routes with three
    different times
All the routes showed construction on the roads
The shortest estimated time of arrival route listed
    one hour and fifteen minutes
I began to get frustrated
I began to think about how my employer would
    complain about my tardiness

I began to sink in my seat not even wanting to
    make the call
I said a quick prayer and took a deep breath
I reached for my phone to make the call
Right before I hit the call button
The GPS began to speak
Then a notification came to my phone with a new
    route
The new route was estimated to get me to my job
    right on time
Lord, thank you for always coming on time

Although you think the wind is working against
you, you will get to your destination on time. Keep
trusting God.

Plowing Pains

God is calling you right now to do something that is impossible. He is calling you to do something that will break generational cycles of lack, defeat, poverty, sickness, and hopelessness from your bloodline. He is calling you to plow for a generation that isn't even here yet. He has chosen and marked you for greatness. Everything on the inside of you was planted for this very reason. There have been many seasons of preparation for you.

You have studied the word, your craft, and strengthened the areas in which you were weak. You have grown in your abilities, your gifts have been nurtured, and your knowledge has expounded. Now you're walking in wisdom with a new-found confidence. There has been an awakening to the mandate on your life. You see whom you're called to. You see the assignments God trusts you with. You see the tests you keep passing. You see the victories you've won. You see all the times where you thought you wouldn't make it but you did. You see all the times you felt as if you were drowning but you were anchored. You see all the times you second guessed if you were capable of greater. You see all the times you placed limitations on God. Now you're in a season called plow.

Like a farmer prepares for harvest, you must first plow. Your plowing in this season will consist of you walking boldly in your purpose. This will involve you planning, leaving, sowing, and growing. You will be assigned to speak life, love, forgive, encourage, educate, edify, affirm, feed, sow, and even pray for those people still on the mountain. Some of these people will see what God is doing in your life and will reach out to you for mental, spiritual, emotional, and even financial help. In this time, don't be moved by emotions but by the Spirit of God.

One cloudy day in October as I drove down Route 30 to pick up one of my clients for our weekly session, I looked over my right shoulder and saw a huge open field, with trees farther in the back. The trees had to have been at least two miles away. As I gazed into this field, the Lord whispered in my ear, giving me clarity and peace regarding my next set of instructions.

This conversation was after God had been dealing with me for the past week about quitting my job. The instructions had been given to me several times throughout the year, but I didn't think I would leave my job that year as my plans were to leave the following year.

When I received word from God that I'd done a great job on my assignment at my job, I was extremely excited. But I was caught off guard because everything changed in one day. God had me walking around singing, and I thought I had at least eight more months left at the job, if not more. I prayed for less time, but I didn't know how things would pan out. I had thought I would transition to another job paying more money so that I could save and invest more into my business. All along, God had another plan.

After working nine straight hours without a break, trying to get everything ready for an audit, I took a break. While sitting in my car, I broke down and cried out to God, expressing how tired I was. I spoke about the hurt and pain I had been enduring, and as I poured out my heart and frustrations in complete vulnerability to God, I told him, "I will do anything for your glory."

God told me, "Daughter, go to your calculator and break down your salary. I want you to see how much they pay you hourly." Without hesitation, I put the numbers in the calculator and did the math. At this point, I had been working there for ten months, but I had never done this calculation. When I accepted the job, the salary was more than the job I was leaving, and I saw that as a win.

When the numbers popped up showing how much I was paid hourly, God said, "Daughter, how much does your business pay you hourly?" I did that calculation, and it was a huge difference. Hourly, my own business paid me almost three times more than my job. This blew my mind. In that moment, something shifted.

To my surprise, the shift didn't come with great excitement. It came with the opposite—great fear. I thought about everything that could possibly go wrong when I quit the job. I thought about not being able to make ends meet. I thought about my businesses possibly failing. The enemy was trying to infiltrate my mind with all the wrong thoughts. I should've been happy in that moment. Didn't I go through hell and work extremely hard to get to this point? Didn't God promise me this? Why was I feeling this way?

Distractions Will Come

Some people, places, and things will be mere distractions. You can't let these throw you off. You must use your discernment and pray to God to reveal all things to you. Distractions are sent from hell to delay and stop us from doing what God has called us to do. We're aware the enemy wants to steal, kill, and destroy us. We have to stay on alert. Let's not get to a place where things are looking good and feeling good, but we get low on our post. We must continue to be on top of things and not slack off. The moment we slack off is the moment when distractions slip through the cracks.

Whether you want to believe it or not, there is a purpose on the inside of you that is leaping to come out. You're PREGNANT WITH A PURPOSE. This is why life gets frustrating; you get sick of things; you get tired, grow weary, want to be lazy, want to give up, and get emotional. It's growing pains. It's all a part of the process. As you grow and mature in your processes, the more people you bring up the mountain with you. Life is lonely when you're at the top by yourself.

Justly, God does not get the glory by changing our lives and forgetting about everyone else's. God does not desire to bless us abundantly and not bless others abundantly. His plans were not to restore our lives and leave others. He used us so that we can be a template to others to show that with Him all things are possible. Get ready to see as you plow what God is going to do in and through your life.

For nothing will be impossible with God (Luke 1:37).

Obstacles Birth Purpose

Over two years ago, I woke up around five in the morning with extreme pain in my back and stomach. The pain would not stop. I remember sitting on the toilet to pee, and after I wiped myself, the tissue turned red. I panicked, not knowing what was going on and what I should do. I ran to my phone and called the closest person I've ever had in my life. I frantically told her what happened. She instructed me to call my doctor.

I took her advice and called my doctor, who suggested I come into emergency as quickly as possible. After hurriedly dressing, I grabbed my keys, phone, and purse, and rushed out the door. I jumped in my car, turned on my worship music, and prayed like never before.

While driving to the hospital, I started moving quickly on the streets, speeding through yellow lights and trying my best to quickly get to my destination. I made a few phone calls to alert people what was going on. At the same time, I looked at my GPS to find the best route to take in the early morning traffic.

The GPS sent me into Lower Wacker Drive. If you're from Chicago, you know how that goes, and it's not good. Your signal drops. This means if you're using a GPS or are on the phone, there is possibly a disconnection or a lag in response. I was on the phone with my mom at the time, and I didn't want to tell her I was on Lower Wacker Drive because I remember when I was a little girl and how she hated driving on that street. She would be in the passenger seat panicking, and I didn't need her panicking more than she already was. However, she asked me where I was, and of course, when I told her, she started fretting and nattering. I politely replied that I was close to the hospital and would see her when she arrived.

When I arrived at the hospital, I was rushed from emergency intake to a room. Shortly after, I was rushed into surgery. In the surgery room, I was told to lie in bed and stretch out my arms so they could strap them to the sides of the bed. They proceeded to give me tons of drugs to dull the pain. These drugs were so strong I was delirious. My room was filled with over thirty doctors, nurses, surgeons, and pediatricians. Everyone was dressed for surgery and called out their names. They checked every scalpel, syringe, knife, blade, cotton ball, and everything else they needed for this moment. They placed a sheet-like material in front of my face so I couldn't see what would happen.

Before I knew it, it was time for me to have an emergency C-section. My bundle of joy was ready to bless the world with her presence. Although I was doped up on medication, I felt the pulling and tugging from the incision. The doctor monitoring me at the head of the bed saw my uncomfortableness. Her job was to make sure I didn't feel anything and to provide me with enough medication to ensure this. So, of course, she kept injecting my IV with medication, and I became even more delirious. I had been praying ever since I had awoken that morning, and in this moment, I prayed even harder. An unexplainable calmness and peace came over me.

And then, before I knew it, I heard the best sound a mother could hear—my baby's first cry. Overwhelming emotions of peace, joy, happiness, love, and the power of God hit me in a new way. As my daughter entered this world, she made sure I was aware of it. I couldn't see her, but she came in just like her momma: loud and making her presence known. All sorts of thoughts swirled around in my head. Was she okay? I wanted to hold her. I wanted to kiss her. I wanted to hug her.

I didn't have contact with her for approximately five minutes. It could have been longer or even shorter than this, but I was delirious. I recall the moment I saw her for the first time. She was the brightest and most beautiful baby I had ever seen. The doctors positioned her on my chest and eventually gave me access to one of my arms. I was able to hug and kiss my beautiful baby girl, Royalty. She was everything a mom could pray for. She was perfect in my eyes. While her life outside of my tummy only lasted for an hour and fifty-eight minutes, the impressions she made on my heart and the impact she made to my life will last for eternity.

The doctors checked her pulse and it wasn't there any longer. They declared her deceased, handed her back to me, and I personally witnessed her soul leave her body as I stared at her in my hands. The day of her death was the beginning of purpose being birthed in my life. God used her to awaken something inside me from the moment I found out I was pregnant. When I became aware I was pregnant with a purpose in the natural, God began to give me revelation about what it means to be pregnant with a purpose spiritually.

Pregnancy in the natural is very closely related to pregnancy in the spiritual. The only difference is that spiritually, males and females are both pregnant with a purpose. There is a seed deep down within all of us that we must give birth to whether we want to or not. During my pregnancy, labor, and delivery, I grew closer to God. One of my cries to God was, "I will do whatever you want me to do, go wherever you want me to go, say whatever you want me to say." I asked for clarity, guidance, and the leading of the Holy Spirit.

I was shown very clearly during this time what my purpose was and to whom I was called. I wasn't given clear directions on how to get there or how to help these people, but the more I pressed into

God and walked out on faith, the more instructions and clarity he provided.

When you're in a season where you lack faith, ambition, understanding, clarity, and finances, you want to give up. You're in pain. You're lonely. You feel as if no one understands. You feel like God has left you. "Why me?" you ask. You say, "If it isn't one thing, it's another."

Trust me. I feel you. I've felt these same things at many places in my life, even during the pregnancy with Royalty. I've learned that if you stay focused on what you don't have and allow your feelings to control you, you will stay in the same place for the rest of your life. Vision is given and great purpose is birthed during the most uncomfortable times.

Instead, think positively and mediate on what God has revealed to you. God has given you glimpses of your future and where He wants to take you and to whom you're called. Now is the time to walk boldly in your purpose, doing what you know you're called to do. God has given you the gifts, talents, abilities, wisdom, experience, resources, and connections to do everything you're called to do.

Today, I reflect with great joy, love, peace, and purpose. I understand why God allowed for this to be my journey. God allowed the scars so I could rescue someone. I'm now in a position in life where I'm completely living in my purpose. I don't sit in sorrow because my daughter died but I intentionally walk in purpose each day.

- One month after my baby girl passed away, I began writing my first book, *Pregnant With a Purpose: Scars Christ Allowed to Rescue Someone.*

- Ten weeks after I started writing this book, I finished it.

- Seven months after my baby girl passed away, my first book was published and I released two new businesses.

- Less than six months after publishing my book and starting my businesses, I released my second book, *Born With a Purpose* (a children's book) and started Sponsor a Child Campaign to help promote literacy, purpose, and identity into the lives of inner-city children. With the help of the community, this allowed me to donate my books and speak to K-3rd graders at Betty Shabazz International Charter School in Chicago.

- Three months after releasing my children's book, I quit my job to work full-time for myself, helping speakers, content creators, aspiring authors, and other entrepreneurs write books in ten weeks so they can walk in their purpose while growing their business.

The above is a brief synopsis of what I've accomplished after suffering the biggest obstacle in my life. I didn't give up on God. I allowed my faith in God to stretch me without limits to birth some things the world needed that were kicking on the inside of me.

Obstacles should birth purpose not poverty. We have to change our minds and actions in response to things. I encourage you to spend time sitting in the presence of God to build a relationship with Him. Ask questions, share your heart, be vulnerable, and receive clarity and direction regarding your next few steps.

What you have access to and what you've overcome are not just for you. They are for the betterment of the people you are called to. I'm sure God has already been giving you revelation as to why you're currently experiencing or have experienced certain things and how it connects to your purpose. The only problem is that you're afraid to step out on faith and walk in your purpose. You feel like you need all the details. You don't! Just go!

That gift? Use it!
That story? Tell i!
That book? Write It!
That blog? Launch it!

That app? Develop it!
That idea? Produce it!
That podcast? Launch it!
That purpose? Walk in it?

One of my greatest gifts from God is the ability to meet new people, converse with them, connect in the spirit, and we feel as if we've known each other for years. My friends make jokes about me always talking to everyone and holding conversations with complete strangers. My mom told me ever since I learned to speak and wave I would say "Hey" and wave to everyone I saw no matter where we went. She mentioned that I even went up to people and gave them hugs.

Over the years, I met thousands of people and took the time to get to know them. Whether it was two minutes or two hours or more, I was intent upon getting to know who they were. I always ask questions and I'm always transparent in conversation. This allows for others to be transparent with me no matter how long we've known each other. Most people have told me, "I feel like I've known you all of my life." This was a comment even after a brief encounter.

One thing I've realized is my ability to build rapport quickly with individuals and plant seeds in them. In these sometimes brief and many times long conversations, I can see who they truly are— who God called them to be and the potential trapped inside of them that they have yet to give birth to due to fear or lack of knowledge. In these moments, I find a way to highlight the things that God reveals to me and encourage them to walk by faith in doing so.

I've met so many individuals who've lost expectation in God for their lives to be all that He said it would be. Some individuals let their environments and current circumstances tell me that God is not who He says He is. "God is not a man, that he should lie, nor a son of man, that he should change his mind. Does he speak and then not act? Does he promise and not fulfill?" (Numbers 23:19, NIV).

We experience trials of many kinds, but God is always with us. He never leaves us nor forsakes us. In the midst of the trials, God is speaking to us. I know you feel confused as to why God is asking you to do something so great. I know you're wondering, *Why me?* The real question is why not you?

Write down what God has recently instructed you to do in the midst of a trial.

_____
_____
_____
_____

Now I want you to take some time to pray about this exact thing God has spoken to you about. Ask God for courage to do what He has instructed you.

Then ask Him when you should do this and what steps you need to take first. Then, with complete confidence, do what God has instructed you to do.

Faith in Action

20You foolish person, do you want evidence that faith without deeds is useless? 21Was not our father Abraham considered righteous for what he did when he offered his son Isaac on the altar? 22You see that his faith and his actions were working together, and his faith was made complete by what he did. 23And the scripture was fulfilled that says, "Abraham believed God, and it was credited to him as righteousness," and he was called God's friend. 24You see that a person is considered righteous by what they do and not by faith alone. 25In the same way, was not even Rahab the prostitute considered righteous for what she did when she gave lodging to the spies and sent them off in a different direction? 26As the body without the spirit is dead, so faith without deeds is dead (James 2:20-26, NIV).

Abraham's life was an example of faith in action. I want to be this example. I want people to look at my life as an example of faith. I want people to say if God has blessed Taneisha because of her faith, then I know He will bless me because of my own.

The key is not to let your environment or obstacles, or lack thereof, throw you off. If you only pay attention to what's in front of you, you will not move at all. You will allow the opposite of faith—

fear—to take over. Fear cripples us and keeps us complacent. You must keep your eyes on God, obey Him, move, and wait for the promises to manifest in your life. God's word never returns void.

Look at your hands. What do you see?

You can't focus on what you don't see in your hands. God has given you everything you need in the palm of your hands. You just don't have the ability to see it in the natural. Ask God to remove the scales from your eyes. Now try looking with your spiritual eyes.

Look around you. What do you see?

You can't focus on what your surroundings look like. It can change in one minute, hour, or day. By faith, you have to see yourself beyond your current place.

Look at your resources and connections. What do you see? You have to see the limitless resources and divine connections that you inherited through Abraham.

You can't focus on the lack thereof. There are blessings with your name on it, waiting for you to unlock them.

What you don't see are mere distractions that will cause you to stay complacent and take your focus from the abundance of God. You must be reminded by Abraham's life that God will fulfill His promises if you obey Him. Trust and wait patiently on God. In the midst of obstacles, have hope and believe in God's promises. When we believe in God, an exchange takes place. We are given the blessing before it happens.

[20]He replied, "Because you have so little faith. Truly I tell you, if you have faith as small as a mustard seed, you can say to this mountain, 'Move from here to there,' and it will move. Nothing will be impossible for you" (Matthew 17:20, NIV).

Faith in action gives us things that once weren't accessible. This requires you to:

- Write down the dreams and visions you see for your life.

- Take one step when you have no idea what all the steps are.

- Reach out and connect with people who God highlights.

- Go to places you've never been because God spoke to you about it.

- Write down words, phrases, and ideas even when they don't make sense.

- Sell everything or pack up and move to a new city.

- Travel to a state, region, or conference that you've never been to.

- Invest into your business and personal development.

- See the ending of something before you've even started.

- Write that business plan and launch that business.
- Share your story with others.

Things that weren't accessible to you before you stepped out in faith become accessible to you. Things such as:

- Wisdom

- Money

- Power

- People

- Influence

- Property

- Environments

- Prestige

- Overflow

Faith in action moves and unlocks things in the spirit realm. Faith brings us to a place of maturation, completeness, and abundance, without lacking anything.

3because you know that the testing of your faith produces perseverance. 4Let perseverance finish its work so that you may be mature and complete, not lacking anything (James 1:3-4, NIV).

Once you remove all limitations that were once placed on God for your lives, you will see the abundance of God. You will see the God of overflow. Faith in action stretches you without limits. When you think about limits, think about a box. When you think about no limits, think about a lake, ocean, the sky, or God. God has no limits and no boundaries. We have full access to Him, so why do we place limits and boundaries on what He can do in and through our lives? Become like Abraham. Let your life be an example of faith in motion. Let people see your life and use it as a template to access the inheritance of "more than enough" from God.

What types of people will you have access to?

_____

_____

_____

_____

What has God called you to do? If you're uncertain, spend time seeking God about this and then write down what He has revealed.

_____

_____

_____

_____

What has God instructed you do for you in the next month?

_____

_____

_____

_____

Write down the abundant life God revealed you will have.

_____

_____

_____

_____

It is Happening

After a few weeks seeking God regarding how and when I needed to leave my job, He gave me the first step to take, as well as when. He told me to do it the right way—to write a notice informing my employer that November 1 would be my last day of work. I wrote the letter and tried my best to find the "perfect time to give it to my boss." God gave me the courage and extra push to "just do it." Since I worked from home four days each week, I sent it in an email. Once the email was sent, a ton of weight left my shoulders and my mind. I couldn't believe I had really done it.

Later that evening, I embarked on a three-hour drive to see a client. On my drive, God gave me peace about my next steps. He told me He would provide no matter what it looked like. He told me He would make my name great. He informed me I would have some good and bad days in entrepreneurship. He told me I would feel the pains of building my companies but not to confuse that with His absence. He told me that greater things were on the way and I would see why it was important to be obedient and how walking blindly by faith would bless all people connected to me.

As of November 1, I was self-employed full-time and have seen the favor of God on my life like never before. He has done everything He told me He would do and even more. I learned the importance of decreeing and declaring the word of God over my life. I have seen things come to past because of the words I spoke by faith. God has continued to provide provision for my next steps. Most of the time, I'm uncertain as to why He is instructing me to do a particular thing and exactly how I need to do it, but my confidence in Him allows me to do it. And God continues to give me confirmation that I'm hearing from Him concerning the directions to take in life. The Bible says in James 4:2, NIV, "you do not have because you do not ask God." Meditate on this for a minute.

At every stage in your life, in every assignment, there is always a new level of faith that is needed. This faith is ignited when you look back over your life and see the pattern of God's faithfulness. Live your life boldly without worries. Don't waste time thinking about what might go wrong. Let your mindset be: If I don't do it, not only will I lack but those who are attached to me will live in lack.

Here is what God wants you to know:

I am bringing you into a new realm of my spirit.

Realm - a kingdom; a field or domain of activity of interest.

I am bringing you into a new dimension of my glory.

Dimension - measurable, extent of some kind, such as length, breadth, depth, or height.

I am taking you to different environments for my glory.

Environment - the social and cultural forces that shape a life of a person or a population.

When you step out in faith, you will experience God taking you into new realms. He will enlarge your borders and take you to places you have never been. He will open up your eyes to new environments with new people. These will be people beyond what you've prayed for. Get ready to sit amongst kings, queens, CEOs, CFOs, COOs, and other people of power and influence. As you come into new territory, you will begin to encounter God in ways that exceed your expectations. God wants you to release all your ideas of what things will be like and believe Him for greater things. Get ready to access new realms, dimensions, environments, people, blessings, and prosperity.

In closing, in all that you do, seek God, obey Him, and wait for Him. Create a vision for your life, write it down, have crazy faith, put it to action, and it will manifest. Remember, you were created to succeed. Continue to walk boldly even when you can't see the promises. The wind will be against you and pressure will come, but allow God to stretch you beyond your limits. This is what produces diamonds. Diamonds shine brightly everywhere they go. Let God mold you into a bright and shining diamond. Declare the promises of God over your life and get full access to your prosperity. Remember, even though you can't see it, believe that it is happening. Let Abraham be the example that your faith in God rewards all people attached to you. Let your faith in God be the example to others that God is a promise keeper and will abundantly exceed all that you ask.

16Therefore, the promise comes by faith, so that it may be by grace and may be guaranteed to all Abraham's offspring—not only to those who are of the law but also to those who have the faith of Abraham. He is the father of us all. 17As it is written: "I have made you a father of many nations." He is our father in the sight of God, in whom he believed—the God who gives life to the dead and calls into being things that were not.

18Against all hope, Abraham in hope believed and so became the father of many nations, just as it had been said to him, "So shall your offspring be." 19Without weakening in his faith, he faced the fact that his body was as good as dead—since he was about a hundred years old—and that Sarah's womb was also dead. 20Yet he did not waver through unbelief regarding the promise of God, but was strengthened in his faith and gave glory to God, 21being fully persuaded that God had power to do what he had promised. [22]*This is why "it was credited to him as righteousness"* (Romans 4:16-22, NIV).

About Taneisha

Taneisha L. Naylor is a writing coach who helps speakers, content creators, and aspiring authors write their first book in ten weeks to help grow their businesses. She is the author of *Pregnant with a Purpose: Scars Christ Allowed to Rescue Someone* and *Born with a Purpose* (a children's book.)

She understands that she was created by God to educate, empower, encourage, and equip men and women through her speeches, books, writing coaching, and God-given gifts. Taneisha's desire is to travel to all nations to speak about her testimony, share the wisdom of God, and to encourage people to walk blindly by faith.

Taneisha graduated from Northern Illinois University with a bachelor's degree in Family Consumer Nutrition Studies with an emphasis in Family Social Services and a minor in Black Studies.

Visit taneishanaylor.net to find more about her.

Contact Taneisha at:

info@taneishanaylor.net